JASON

Saves the Environment
with Entrepreneurship

Words by Erica Swallow
Pictures by Li Zeng

Entrepreneur
Kid

To Li and all who venture to chase the American dream.
— E.S.

To my loving American family: Rick and Sharman, Tommy and Belinda.
— L.Z.

Text copyright © 2017 Erica Swallow ● Illustrations copyright © 2017 Li Zeng ● All rights reserved. Published in 2017 by Entrepreneur Kid in Redwood City, CA 94065. ● No portion of this book may be reproduced, stored in a retrieval system, or transmitted in any form or by any means, mechanical, electronic, photocopying, recording, or otherwise, without written permission from the publisher. For permissions, write to hi@entrepreneurkid.com. ● Printed in China. ● Library of Congress Cataloging-in-Publication Data ● Names: Swallow, Erica, author. | Zeng, Li, 1988-, illustrator. ● Title: Jason saves the environment with entrepreneurship / by Erica Swallow ; illustrated by Li Zeng. ● Series: Entrepreneur Kid. ● Description: Redwood City, CA: Entrepreneur Kid, 2017. ● Identifiers: ISBN 978-1-946984-02-9 (Hardcover) | 978-1-946984-08-1 (pbk.) | 978-1-946984-09-8 (ebook) | LCCN 2017939661 ● Summary: Jason Li has been on a mission to pay for his own lunch; his idea helps him do just that while saving the planet. ● Subjects: LCSH Li, Jason. | Young businesspeople--Juvenile literature. | Businesspeople--United States--Biography--Juvenile literature. | Entrepreneurship--Juvenile literature. | Small business--Juvenile literature. | Recycling (Waste, etc.)--Juvenile literature. | Sustainable living--Juvenile literature. | Electronics--Juvenile literature. ● BISAC JUVENILE NONFICTION / General | JUVENILE NONFICTION / Business & Economics | JUVENILE NONFICTION / Careers | JUVENILE NONFICTION / Recycling & Green Living ● Classification: LCC HC102.5. L5 2017 | DDC 338.04/092--dc23 ● Printed in China ● First printing, June 2017 ●The text type was set in Capriola Regular and NTR. ● The display text was set in Passero One and Arial Rounded MT Bold. ● The illustrations were created using Adobe Illustrator. ● Special thank you to design interns Logan Melton and Shiori Soya for assistance with art.

Jason Li and his family moved to the United States when he was four years old.

When he first arrived, everyday life was confusing. Everyone around him spoke English, but he only spoke Chinese. He would use his big, red dictionary to look up words he had never heard.

As he grew, Jason realized he wanted to give back to his parents for giving him all he needed.

"I want to figure out how to make at least three dollars every day," he told his parents one day as they planted trees at the local park. "That way, I can pay for my own lunch!"

Little did Jason know, he would grow up to learn not only the language of the country, but also how to build a business and give back to his community.

Jason thought of many ideas of how to earn his lunch money. First, he drew comic strips and sold them to his friends. But drawing was tough, and he didn't feel that art was his specialty.

Then, he started a clothing line. He asked his classmates if they would buy t-shirts with funny sayings on them. Everyone thought it was a great idea!

After he printed the shirts, though, no one bought them. He had borrowed money from his parents for the shirts, so he felt extra bad that the business didn't work.

In middle school, Jason noticed that his friends started using cell phones. Some of his classmates even got new ones every year.

Jason wondered, "Where do all the old electronics go when people get new ones?"

E-WASTE

In his World Geography class, Jason learned that many phone parts harm the environment and can't be recycled. Those parts are sent to countries like China and Ghana, where they destroy land and water streams, making life hard for locals.

Jason remembered his childhood in China and was shocked. He wondered if people knew the harm their phones created for others far, far away.

That year, he got his first music player.

His parents were excited to surprise him with it, but within two weeks, he dropped it and broke the screen. Jason felt horrible!

Jason didn't want his parents to know he had ruined it.
So, he researched how to fix broken music players. He
found lots of resources and bought the ones he needed.

"I did it!" he exclaimed one day. With his new tools, Jason fixed his music player!

Disaster averted.

Jason's classmates were impressed. Kids from all over campus asked him to fix their phones.

"Hey, I have a business here!" Jason thought. "Maybe I could find more people who need my help."

iReTron

Green for the enviroment.
Green for your wallet.

Recycling Phones
Contact:Jason Li
123 456 7890

Jason posted ads everywhere. People from all over town called him. They liked the idea of recycling their phones. Jason would buy, repair, and resell the phones.

He was saving the environment while also making money. He started paying for his own lunches at school!

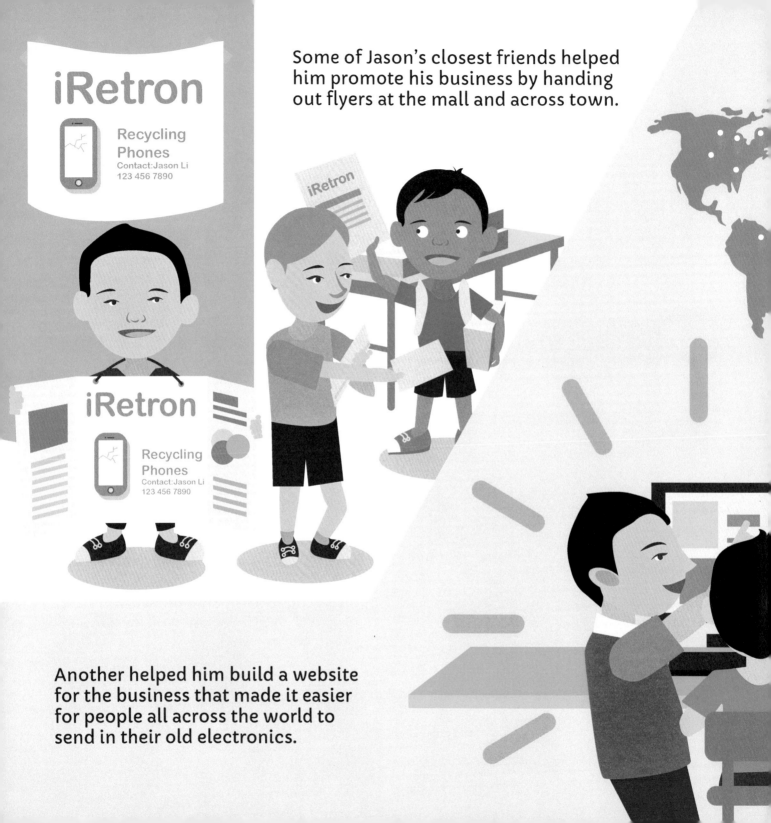

iRetron

Recycling
Phones
Contact:Jason Li
123 456 7890

Some of Jason's closest friends helped him promote his business by handing out flyers at the mall and across town.

iRetron

Recycling
Phones
Contact:Jason Li
123 456 7890

Another helped him build a website for the business that made it easier for people all across the world to send in their old electronics.

Two more friends helped him make a video that explains how the website works. With that video, they won a national teen business competition!

Jason was grateful that his friends were so supportive.

Jason's parents were a big inspiration while he was starting his business, too. His dad drove him EVERYWHERE for business meetings and speaking events. He was more than a dad on those drives; he was a business advisor!

His mom started a business that year, too. She was a Chinese teacher and decided to open her own Chinese school. When Jason went to bed, his mom was always awake making plans for the school. When he woke up, she was always there making breakfast and sending him off to school. He was certain she had super powers.

Not everyone supported Jason's creativity, though. One of his classmates told him every day that he'd never be successful. Some parents even thought his goals were too ambitious.

They were right that it was tough to be a student while starting a business. But Jason wanted to prove that he could do it.

And he did! One eventful day, Jason was on a popular TV show where real investors give promising entrepreneurs money to grow their businesses.

All of the other business owners on the show were much older than him. He was worried that he was too young to impress the investors.

"Don't worry, kid," the TV producer told him. "That's what makes you stand out. Be yourself!" That was exactly what he needed to hear.

The investors loved his idea and that he had started a business while so young. They invested! From then on, Jason started to embrace himself as he was.

That year, Jason learned that he had inspired some of his classmates to start their own businesses.

Vivian

Designed personalized notebooks

Cody

Started a graphic design company

Kristen

Founded a photography business

He also got into college to continue his education and hired three people to keep the business running while he was away at school.

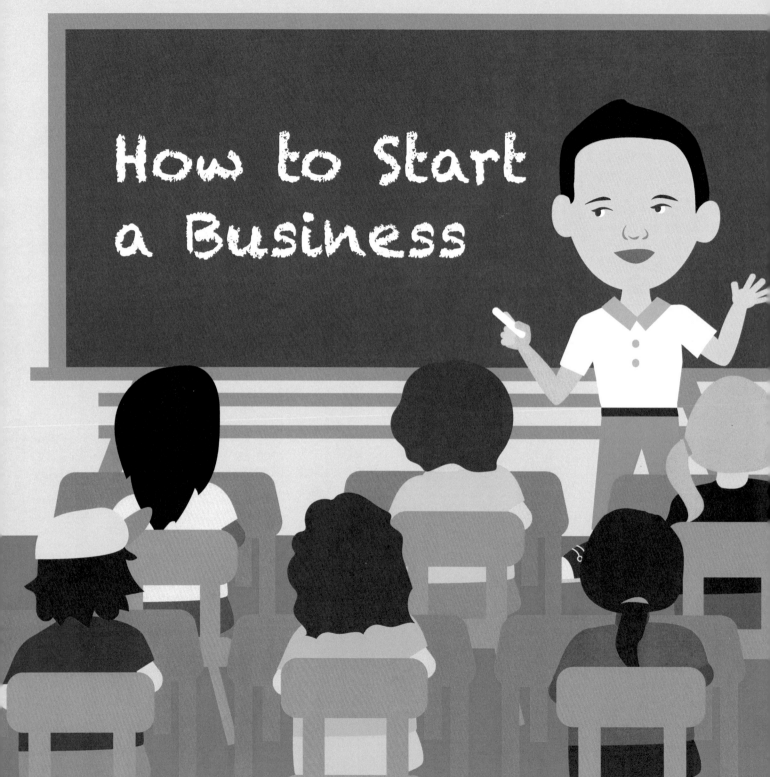

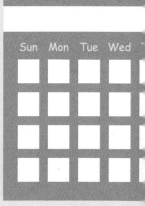

Jason Li

Jason now helps other kids become entrepreneurs.

He visits local high schools to teach, and his high school back home has a special class for kids who want to start businesses, like he did.

In college, Jason even started a program that trains his classmates on how to start businesses!

Jason's company helps the environment while also helping pay for his education. He never has to ask his parents for lunch money again!

In fact, sometimes he even treats his mom and dad to lunch!

Jason says his key to success is embracing who he really is. He didn't know how to speak English when he arrived in the United States, and he knew nothing about business. But he learned along the way. You can, too!

Don't be afraid to embrace who you really are. You can do anything you put your mind to!

Now it's your turn...
What problems do you want to solve in the world?

Author's Note by Erica Swallow

"Jason Saves the Environment with Entrepreneurship" is the story of teen entrepreneur Jason Li, who at the age of 14 founded iReTron, a social enterprise that buys, refurbishes, resells, and donates used electronics.

Jason's interest in starting iReTron was sparked when he learned about electronic waste, or "e-waste" in his ninth grade World Geography class. He was astonished to learn that electronics — such as computers, phones, and televisions — end up in large garbage dumps in countries including Ghana, India, and China, where he was born. In "e-waste villages," old electronics are separated for scrap metals and the unusable plastics and waste are burned, wreaking havoc on the local environment and for the people, animals, and vegetation nearby. Jason wanted to fix the problems e-waste introduced.

The young entrepreneur also had a second motive for starting his business. At around 10 years old, Jason began to realize the hard work and sacrifice his parents, Weidong Li and Hui Shen, put into raising him and his younger sister, Jennifer. They immigrated to the United States when Jason was only four years old and Jennifer was not yet born. He told me during an interview that even the smallest tasks could be daunting in those times. He remembers studying a big red dictionary with his mother, because the two of them didn't speak English when they arrived. He and I had a good laugh in that interview when he recalled a time he spent 30 minutes looking up a Pokémon character name, Bulbasaur, in the dictionary. He says he was so angry he couldn't find it. But that's determination right there!

Jason's persistence shows through in his entrepreneurial story, too. In fourth grade, he set a goal to try to make $3.00 per day, so he could pay for

Jason Li and friends promote iReTron. Photo: iReTron

his own school lunch, to show his parents he was grateful for all they had done. He drew and sold comic books, then started a t-shirt business. Neither took off.

One fateful day, Jason broke his iPod Touch, a handheld computing device his parents had given him just weeks prior. As any kid would, he went into panic mode to try to fix it before his parents found out. He learned he could repair the device by ordering a replacement screen online. The fix was a success. Coupling his newfound repair knowledge with his passion for the environment, Jason realized he could help others recycle and resell their old or broken devices.

Jason's business started small, at Saratoga High School, where he fixed classmates' electronics. He expanded by posting ads online, and his friends helped him promote the business at the local mall and nearby events. Soon, adults were buying Jason's services, too, but he wanted to go big. As a freshman in high school, Jason paid a family friend in pizza to help him build a website that would automate the buying and selling process. They launched the site, iReTron.com, in November 2011, when Jason was a sophomore. From there, business took off.

Financially, iReTron started with a $2,000 loan from Jason's dad. The company then began to win business competitions, pulling in $43,000 in prize money. Finally, in 2014, at 16 years old, Jason took the stage on ABC's *Shark Tank*, leaving with an investment of $100,000 from Barbara Corcoran and Mark Cuban. That year, iReTron earned $2 million in revenue.

Today, the company continues to operate out of Jason's hometown of Los Gatos, California. He hired three employees to manage shipments and repairs while he studies at the University of Chicago, where he is majoring in Economics and Computer Science and teaches fellow students about entrepreneurship through a startup accelerator he helped launch.

Jason has accomplished a lot in his first two decades of life. In 2015, Jason spoke at TEDxUChicago about everyday entrepreneurship. He led iReTron to victory at the Students for the Advancement of Global Entrepreneurship (SAGE) National Competition and "Next Teen Tycoon" competition in 2012. He has even given entrepreneurship another shot while in college, founding a second company called UProspie, focused on making higher education more accessible to students from all backgrounds. Jason expects to graduate from the University of Chicago in 2017 at 20 years old.

While writing this book, illustrator Li Zeng, videographer Dan Ndombe, and I visited Jason and his family. The story and illustrations you've encountered in this book were all inspired by in-person and online interviews with the family. To learn more about Jason and his company, visit entrepreneurkid.com and iReTron.com. Both sites feature videos, photos, and more information about the making of iReTron and the Entrepreneur Kid book about the company's beginnings.

iReTron appears on TV show *Shark Tank*. Photo: ©American Broadcasting Companies, Inc.

The Li family. Photo: Dan Ndombe

How many Entrepreneur Kid books have you read?

There are four books in the Entrepreneur Kid series. Read them all to learn how other kids like you started their own businesses. You, too, can be an Entrepreneur Kid by solving problems around you.

Go to entrepreneurkid.com to buy the full series and submit your Entrepreneur Kid story for an opportunity to be featured on our website!

Find Entrepreneur Kid on social media to share your reading experience.

@EntrepreneurKid   @EntrepreneurKid   /EntrepreneurKid   /company/EntrepreneurKid

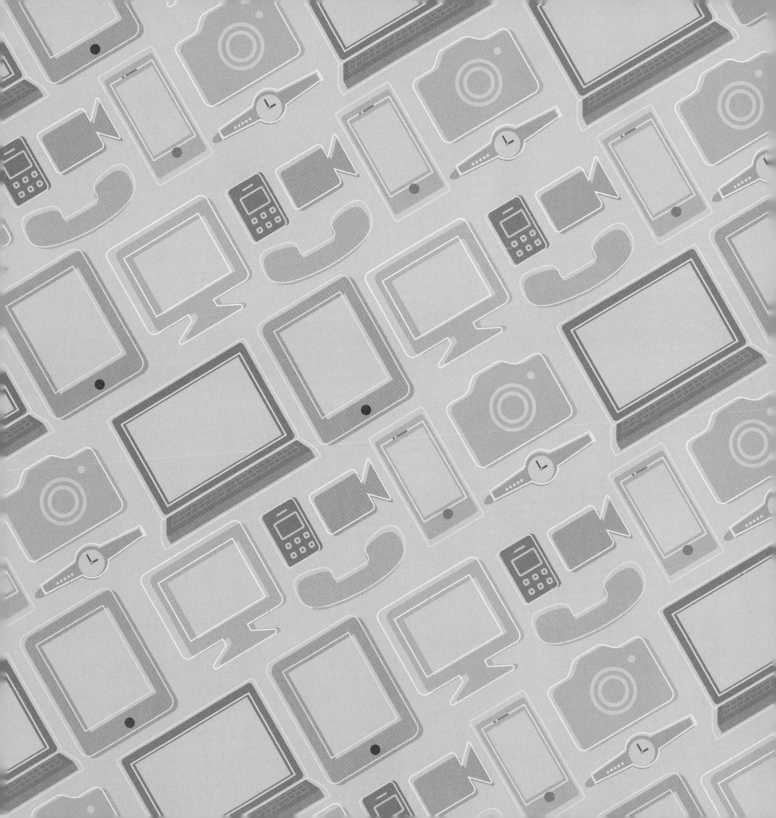

Go to sellbackyourBook.com
and get an instant price
quote. We even pay the
shipping - see what your old
books are worth today!

Inspected By: Emily_Ruiz

00070805847

Made in the USA
Lexington, KY
20 August 2017